The Forbidden
Rumi

The Forbidden
Rumi

The Suppressed Poems of Rumi
on Love, Heresy, and Intoxication

Translations and commentary by
NEVIT O. ERGIN and WILL JOHNSON

Inner Traditions
Rochester, Vermont

Inner Traditions
One Park Street
Rochester, Vermont 05767
www.InnerTraditions.com

Library of Congress Cataloging-in-Publication Data

[to come]

Printed and bound in XXXXX

10 9 8 7 6 5 4 3 2 1

Text design and layout by Priscilla Baker
This book was typeset in Goudy Oldstyle, with Centaur used as a display typeface

To send correspondence to the author of this book, mail a first-class letter to the
author c/o Inner Traditions • Bear & Company, One Park Street, Rochester, VT
05767, and we will forward the communication.

Contents

Songs to Shams, Songs to God

Songs of Advice, Songs of Admonition

Songs of Heresy

Introduction

*H*eretics of the world, take heart. There is a place set for
you at the table of religion after all. In fact, the very finest
delicacies and best wines offered at that table may even be
reserved for you alone to enjoy. The orthodox clerics, the high priests,
the reasonable-minded fathers and mothers of the churches, mosques,
synagogues, and ashrams of the world may all make their way to that
table, but find the fare on their plates and the wine in their glasses a bit
scanty, underwhelming, even a little bland compared with yours.

The orthodox mothers and fathers of religion are pillars of faith
and belief, and they inspire others by their obvious piety. But for you,
O heretics, faith and belief alone are like painted cakes that cannot
satisfy the hunger and yearning you feel in your belly and your heart
and your soul. For you, nothing less than the immediate and direct
experience of what might be called God will do. You need to put it
right in your mouth, taste it, chew it (slowly), and then spend time
digesting it, feeling it, becoming it, before you can find the satisfaction

you seek. And one great meal will not do it for you, either. You need to eat and drink and feast on the divine every chance you get. Your stomach for God is bottomless!

Orthodoxy is what happens to a heresy that becomes institutionalized. All of our founding mothers and fathers of religion have had direct experiences of being split wide open (what the Sufis call *faraji*) and transported into a parallel dimension of consciousness that feels intimately connected with everything that is, rather than estranged and separate from it. Depending on the perspective we embody in the moment, we become aware of a larger energy we may call God, or we stay contained in a very small vessel that we mostly call "me." The true religious journey is one that breaks free of that small vessel and realizes, in every cell of the body, that the larger energy is also what I am.

Orthodoxies everywhere unintentionally but inevitably transform the original heresy into an object of worship, rather than an experience to have. At this point, in the words of Carl Jung, "Organized religion becomes a defense against having the religious experience."

Even so, there have always been renegades within the orthodox traditions, mystics who have penetrated the orthodox teachings back to their original source, heretics who have dispensed with the teachings altogether. Of course, the ultimate heresy is not only to contact the great source that we call God, but also to become so immersed in that source that the only logical proclamation to make is that you and God are one. Here's where the problem begins, for the heretic's truth can make the orthodox believer very uncomfortable. Jesus didn't exactly fare too well for his proclamations. Neither did Mansour al-Hallaj, a tenth-century Sufi saint who was put to death for being foolish enough to declare that he had become the truth.

In this respect Rumi, the great thirteenth-century mystic, poet, and originator of the dance of the whirling dervish, fared considerably better. He was, in fact, a heretic revered.

Rumi's conversion from orthodox Islamic cleric into ecstatic dancer, heretic, and passionate lover of God came about through his chance encounter with an older, wandering dervish named Shams of Tabriz. The two men are reported to have met on a roadway. Something extraordinary was exchanged between them through their glance, and, throwing both their lives and decorum to the winds, they went off together into a closed-door retreat, emerging several months later in a state of ecstatic illumination familiar to the Sufi tradition. Through the prolonged power of their gaze and the exploration of intentional movements, Rumi and Shams dissolved the confining bubbles of separation that ordinarily encase us and mesmerize us into believing that who we are is an entity named "I" that lives inside our individual body and remains separate from everything that exists outside the body. Pop the bubble and you find yourself swimming in a consciousness that perceives itself as merged with the ultimate source of existence. The Sufis call this the consciousness of union, the healing antidote to the fear and alienation that pervade the far more common consciousness of separation.

After being split wide open through the explosive encounter with his great friend Shams, Rumi let go of many of the precepts of formal religion, insisting instead that only a complete personal dissolving into the larger energies of God can provide the satisfaction that the heart so desperately seeks. It is a testament to how well loved Rumi was in his adopted community of Konya, Turkey, that he encountered no reprisals for pronouncements that would almost certainly have gotten him into very hot water indeed had they been uttered instead in present day Iran or in Afghanistan under the Taliban.

As a result of his overwhelming and truly life-altering encounter with Shams, Rumi began to speak spontaneously in the language of poetry, and he spoke and spoke and spoke some more. In total, his poems comprise some forty-four thousand verses, which subsequent compilers organized into twenty-three individual volumes called the *Divan-i-Kebir*. In the pages of these many volumes are to be found some of the most gorgeous expressions that have ever been uttered about the individual soul's ecstatic return to the embrace of God.

Now, it may come as a surprise to lovers of Rumi's poetry to learn that he, in fact, never "wrote" a single poem, not in the way we ordinarily think of writing poetry, anyway. You see, Rumi never actually wrote anything. He simply went about town, unable to keep his ecstasy contained, uttering spontaneous couplets and meters about the dissolution of the soul into the divine embrace of God, ranting and raving, singing out to whomever would listen. He never actually sat down, collected his thoughts, and composed poems in the traditional sense. Nor did he ever work on the poems once they had been uttered. There was no changing of words here, moving of phrases there. With Rumi, the first expression became the final poem.

Fortunately for us, a select circle of friends and students recorded all the poems. These Secretaries of the Scribe, as they became known, wrote down everything to come out of their teacher's mouth, and thanks to them, we still have access to Rumi's actual words.

Unfortunately for us, the compilers did not just list the poems in the chronological order in which they were uttered. Instead, they sorted and collated them according to their poetic structure and meter and even at times according to their subject matter. What this means is that we can't view the poems as a historical document tracing the flow of events in Rumi's life, reflecting the progression and development of his thoughts and ideas. In a single volume you may have poems from the early part of his life following upon poems that were uttered in his later years.

When making your way through the many volumes of the *Divan-i-Kebir,* it is helpful to keep in mind that the written record often reads more like a series of journal entries than it does discrete poems. Every entry chronicles a day during which Rumi would move about town, stopping here to converse with the lovers of God, halting there to admonish the doubters and naysayers, coming to a complete stop as he would go off into ecstasy and bring back word pictures from the other world. All of these things may have happened during a single stroll about town, and so all of them might find their way into a single entry. In the volume of poetry that you hold in your hands, the translators have attempted to free many of the individual poems from the longer journal entries inside which they've been hidden all these years.

The second thing to know about these poems is the story of intrigue that has kept them from finding their way to their audience in the West. Over the past several years, Rumi has become perhaps the most popular poet in the Western world, and the source of this extraordinary explosion of interest in a previously obscure thirteenth-century Islamic mystic can be traced to a small handful of doors. Behind one of these doors lives a delightful Turkish-born surgeon named Nevit Ergin. As a young man in his twenties, Nevit fell under Rumi's spell, and he decided to commit himself to a task that most of his friends and colleagues told him was impossible: He decided to translate the entire

Divan-i-Kebir of Rumi into English, all forty-four thousand verses and twenty-three volumes worth! Until this decision, the number of Rumi poems that had been translated into English could be counted in the low hundreds, not in the tens of thousands.

To support him in his work, Nevit enlisted the help of the government of Turkey. Rumi spent most of his life, after all, in what is present-day Turkey. One can still visit his funeral shrine in Konya. The Mevlevi order of dervish dancers that Rumi's son founded after his father's death is still active in Turkey. The Turkish government was happy to participate, and over a period of fifteen years twenty-two of the original twenty-three volumes were printed by the Society for Understanding Mevlana. (The wonderful translations of Rumi that most of us know and love are, as often as not, reworkings of Nevit's original translations.) With only one more volume to go, Nevit's impossible dream was very close indeed to being fully realized.

And then a strange thing happened. The Turkish government withdrew its support and refused to participate in the publication of the final volume.

The last volume of Rumi's poems has always posed problems, even to the original compilers. Like the kitchen drawer that collects all the odds and ends that have no place of their own, the last volume was where the compilers sent all the entries and poems they didn't know what to do with or that disturbed them. In the first place, these were poems that broke the rules of both poetic meter and content. Rumi would often say that he hated the rules of meter and phrasing in which the poetry of the time was supposed to be composed: so many syllables here, so many lines there. In many of the poems in this last volume, Rumi just cuts loose, wielding words and thoughts in an almost free-form shuffle that sounds more like an enlightened street rapper from the 1990s than a scholarly thirteenth-century poet who would have been expected to construct poems only in the acceptable meters of his time.

Even more than this, though, the compilers must have been troubled by the content of some of the poems. Many of them find Rumi at his most divinely drunken, almost slurring his words, ranting and raving about the great ecstatic game, behaving in a most unorthodox way for an Islamic sheikh. In some of the poems, Rumi fulminates over the stupidities and prejudices of the townsfolk who couldn't accept or even see the extraordinary transformation that had occurred in him because of his association with Shams, and he doesn't mince words. Rumi could swear and curse with the best of them, but he always does it in the most beautiful way.

And then there are the poems that must have stopped the devout Islamic compilers dead in their tracks. What is one to do with poems that refer to Muhammad as "yesterday's man," others that proclaim that love is the only precept of religion and suggest that an unbeliever can't be considered an infidel if he's been the latest victim of love? What is one to do with phrases and verses that exhort people to become heretics if they want to reach the truth in Islam? How can an Islamic teacher actually declare that Jews, Christians, Muslims, and Zoroastrians are all equal in the great heretical game of dissolving into God?

While Rumi remained a devout Muslim throughout his life, he was nonetheless a beacon to all people, regardless of the religious tradition into which they had been born. He exhorted everyone to descend into the great heresy, to experience for themselves their union with all that is. Experience that union, and you shatter and annihilate yourself.

But out of that shattering and annihilation a whole new consciousness can give birth to itself and arise, like the mythical phoenix that often appears in Rumi's poems, out of the ashes of your old self.

Rumi offers revelation, not consolation. He is not here to hold your hand and make you feel better about the trap into which you've been born. That is the job of religion. It is not the path of the heretic.

So many of the wonderful Rumi translations that are currently available have focused on Rumi's optimistic vision, on the joys of the path of love and the rewards of giving yourself to God. This is all well and good, of course, but it only represents one part of what Rumi was actually telling us. Yes, the path of falling into love with the divine gives pleasure and bliss beyond anything you may have previously known, but it also comes with a shadow side. Love can also be a cruel and cold-hearted taskmaster, a cur in heat. Once it has infected your heart, it ravages you, and you are no longer the master or mistress of your life. The loss of affection (which Rumi experienced in an overwhelming way after Shams got up and walked out one day, and again after he left for a final time and was murdered) can be as gut wrenching in its horror as the appearance of a new love can be over-the-top joyous.

As Rumi says, love hits everybody—if one is lucky and open enough, that is. It completely throws life into a spin, but what a spin it is! What will today bring? Another roller coaster ride of love in which moments of ecstatic weightlessness alternate with horrifying dips and drops that leave your stomach in your throat? Love is not just cream on the peaches. It will leave you roughed up and bruised as well. And yet all of us on the path of love need to go through its dark nights if we truly want to witness the beautiful first lights of morning.

Yet who can follow the path to divine love when the goal is to so merge your sense of self with the greater energies of God that you, not surprisingly, become annihilated in the process? The words Rumi dispenses are not sugar wafers of comfort and consolation, nor does he suggest that anyone should ever be satisfied with a single sip of divine wine. He is, rather, completely uncompromising in his insistence that entering into a condition of absence—in which the individual sense of self, like salt dropped into the sea, becomes lost through its merger with the greater energies—is the only way to come out of the suffering and pain that plague us. Furthermore, he insists that this dissolution into the greater is our natural state, the place in which we are most comfortable. This state is the place we are trying to get back to.

Who will throw themselves willingly into divine fire? Divine or not, it's still going to burn. To help us in this venture, Rumi enlists the aid of the cupbearer, the person who keeps pouring divine wine into the mouths of all the heretics and drunks. And he exhorts this cupbearer to keep pouring more and more and more until he totally passes out of himself. Rumi wants us all to become divine alcoholics. Get drunk on the divine energies that course through our bodies. Drink them in, fill yourself until you can stand up no longer, and then drink some more. When it comes to imbibing the divine, enough is not enough. Drink to excess, and then you may suddenly be able to see the kingdom of God clearly, no longer blurred, vague, and out of focus.

Think of these poems as songs more than as poems. Listen to them as though some exalted, spiritual being were composing songs on the spot and singing them just for you. Really listen to the words. Like all great songwriters, Rumi can create whole stories with just a few lines of lyrics. Read the songs like personal oracles that speak to your situation in life. Read the songs slowly. Better yet, sing them aloud to your lover! So much meaning is contained within their simple words. Don't be in a hurry.

So, heretics, take heart. What a friend you have in Rumi! He's one of you. He couldn't follow the rules either. He needed something more than what the orthodox teachings were capable of delivering. Isn't that true of you as well? Let your body be your temple; enter in there, keep going further, down through its maze of corridors and courtyards. Explore every inch of its sensation and thought. Find out for yourself what is true for you. May these poems be a guide and comfort to all the spiritual misfits of the world, those of us who perhaps lost our way following the more orthodox precepts of religion and are looking for another source of inspiration as we continue on our journey.

WILL JOHNSON
MAPLE BAY, BRITISH COLUMBIA
MAY 2005

Songs to Shams, Songs to God

What a story! You finally meet someone in whose presence you are transported to God. You immediately go off together, hand in hand, and shut yourself off from the world behind the closed doors of your retreat room. Over the weeks and months to follow, you dissolve into each other through simply sitting in each other's presence, gazing raptly at each other. (When God sits down before you, where else would you want to look?) When you emerge from your retreat, you are fundamentally different from the person who entered it so many months before.

The only sane thing to do after an event like this is to live happily ever after, yes? But it wasn't like that.

Rumi may have entered into retreat with Shams as a kind of devout shepherd, looking after his flock of followers, but he emerged as a hungry wolf, exhorting people to drop their pretenses, move beyond their rigid adherence to the outward forms of religion, and enter instead into a direct experience of God.

Rumi wanted the townspeople of Konya to recognize Shams as he had come to know and see him: as a direct conduit to the divine. For Rumi, Shams was a funnel that led to God. Exposed to the heat of Shams' presence, Rumi would simply melt, and the mixture of the two souls would take both into the consciousness of union. This is what true religion is all about, and Rumi fully expected his former followers to leap into the divine fire with him.

Their response instead was to react mostly with criticism and outrage to the perceived heresy of two souls merging into the one God. For the orthodox mind, it is accepted that the founder of the religion would have had a direct encounter with the energies of God, but not, evidently, anyone else. The negativity around the companionship between Rumi and Shams grew so large that Shams had no choice but to leave, and Rumi fell apart with grief.

He began to write letters to Shams, begging him to return, and dispatched them to different parts of the Islamic world in the hopes that one of them might eventually be received. More than a year passed before he heard anything back. Yes, Shams would return.

The two great friends immediately plunged back into retreat, and a new round of dissolving and merging of souls began. The reactions of the townspeople continued much the same as before. This time, when Shams left, he was set upon like a hated predator and murdered.

The complete *Divan-i-Kebir* is considered to contain all the spontaneous utterances that Rumi ever made concerning his interaction with Shams. Some of the poems in the selection that follows read like open letters to Shams. Some read like a historical recounting of their time together. Some of them praise Shams as God's representative on Earth, while others rail in anguish at the cruelty of his teasing and the petulance of his departures.

Is Rumi addressing Shams alone in these poems? Or is he directly addressing God? The lines become blurred.

He Took Me Under His Arm

I was dead, but came back to life.
I was the cry, but I became the smile.
Love came and turned me
into everlasting glory.

Here's how it happened:

He said to me, "You don't belong in this house.
You're not nearly crazy enough."
I went and became raving mad
and bound myself in chains.

He said to me, "You're not drunk. Get lost.
You're not from this land."
I went and got pie-eyed drunk
and filled my life with music and dance.

He said to me, "You've never annihilated yourself
so music and dance can't touch you."
I passed out of myself right in front of him
and fell to the ground.

He said to me, "You're a sensible, learned man,
full of reflections and opinions."
I became a silly fool and cut myself off from people.

He said to me, "You're a candle,
the light to these people."
I gave them all up.
I became smoke and spread myself around.

He said to me, "You're the sheikh, the head,
the one who walks at the front, the guide."
I told him that I'm neither sheikh nor guide.
I am the follower of your order.

He said to me, "You have arms and wings.
I don't give anything to you."
I told him that I desire his wings so that
I can cut mine.

His glory then spoke to me and said,
"Don't give up now. You're almost there.
I'll soon grant you the favor you seek and come
    to you."

And so he said to me, "O old love of mine,
Don't ever get out from under my arm."
And I said, "Yes," and I stayed there.

Split Wide Open

You are the essence of the Sun.
I'm only the shadow of the willow tree.
When you shine down upon my head,
I get shorter, melt, and disappear.

My heart found the spark of life,
then split wide open.
My heart found your satin
and gave up this worn, patched cloth.

The embodied soul
was talking about glances and vision
in the early dawn.
I was but a slave who became a landholder
and then turned into the sultan who has everything.

I Won't Repent His Love

A gazelle appeared on this plain.
His eyes started fires everywhere.
Everyone, on horse or on foot,
ran after him to catch him.

They attacked once or twice,
but he disappeared before their eyes.
So fast did he vanish that
he didn't even leave a smell behind.

They started to turn back,
but he appeared again.
They were surprised.

They attacked again.
The gazelle escaped so fast that
even the wind couldn't touch him.

This appearance and disappearance
disturbed the people so much
that they all became obsessed with catching him.
But they got caught up in separation
and fell into the trap of loneliness.

One of them dashed off
but grabbed the ear of a rabbit by mistake.
Another ran toward Baghdad
after a mountain goat.

The crowd separated into two.
One group still expected
to see the gazelle.
The other just wanted to be free
from this trouble.

The gazelle appeared to the ones
who longed to see it
when they passed out beyond themselves.

To the best ones of that group,
the gazelle taught
some verses from the Koran
with his own drunken eyes.

They began to learn the ways
of the gazelle,
and began to act in accordance with them.

With his grace,
he showed his beauty to them.
He not only pointed out the right direction,
he also made them feel better about themselves.

Every other day,
the gazelle would appear
in strange and different dresses.

His strange appearance
shocked and scared them.

In truth, people have
very little tolerance and courage.

Even the earth and sky scare people
if they see in them attributes of the Creator.

Who is this gazelle?
He is the symbol of Shamseddin:
He is my savior, he is my master.
He is the one who came to my rescue
before I even asked for it.

I won't ever repent his love,
even if thousands of the pious advise me to do so.

He is the essence of vision,
the refuge for wisdom.
He is the one
who gives focus to the soul's eye.

Remember, so long as you are here with us,
it's not permissible
to mention anyone else.

There are so many sultans
from the land of Tabriz.
But no one like him
has ever been born.

How Can I Fool Him?

Mind says:
"I fool him with words."
Love says:
"Be silent.
I trick him with heart and soul."

Soul says to heart:
"Go away. Don't make me laugh.
Everything is his already,
So how could I cheat him with anything?

"He's not someone
who's fallen into thought
hoping to forget himself,
so that I might distract him
with wine and large glasses."

The arrow of his glance
doesn't need a bow from me
in order to hit the target.

He's like a house that
startles angels with its ornaments.
Where could I find better ones
to dazzle him?

He doesn't need horses.
He flies without wings.

He eats and drinks divine light.
How could I buy him off with a bit of bread?

He's the merchant of the universe,
but he buys and sells nothing.
How could I cheat him with profits and losses?

Nothing can be kept secret from him.
How could I pretend to be ill
by moaning, "Unghhhhhhhh, unghhhhhhhh?"
How could I fool him?

I could tie my head
in vinegar-soaked bandages.
I could cry out, "I'm dying."
I wouldn't get his attention or pity.

He knows everything about me,
hair by hair.
What doesn't he know
that I might cheat him with?

He's not after fame
or poets who praise him so that
I might fool him
with verses, ghazals,* and poems.

Shams of Tabriz is his chosen one, his beloved.
I may be able to influence him with that.

———
*A poem constructed of several two-line stanzas.

Water

Since you are the keeper of our soul,
throw our soul in the water
like the cradle of Moses.

Throw, so that neither pharaoh nor the evil people
would be able to find him.

His beautiful cradle will float free
of any fear or desperation
and keep swaying in the water.

If he can't reach the water,
the pharaoh would recognize him.

You are master of this water,
and the water is always around you.
You are the source of the water.
Brilliantly bright, strong and powerful,
water gets its beauty and fluidity from you.

Moses was kept at home
out of fear for his life.
But it was in water that he found his salvation.

Everything is alive with water.
Water is like an appetizer
that drops from the sky.

Stay with Me

Don't go home.
Stay with me tonight.
Little by little, slowly but surely,
my breath will lead you
to insanity.
You'll be freed from the mind.
Then suddenly you'll go crazy.

You follow your fancy,
come to me,
and decide to leave?
What a shame.
What a disgrace.
Is your bond no stronger than this?

Worse than that,
if gold came to find you,
what a great mistake that would be.
You don't deserve any gold,
not even gold the size of a kernel of barley.

Don't run because you fear death.
Run in order to get somewhere.
O my soul, run to reach the sacred place,
not because you fear the Bedouin.

Stay with me every night until dawn.
One evening you'll see the rising moon
that will free you from your journey
and the bad company you've been keeping.

Anyone can see the moon's face from a distance.
How lucky is the one who takes the moon hostage.

Like the sun, the moon too
threatens you at the beginning.
He draws his sword:
"If you don't get away from here,
I'll cut off your head!"

But when he sees that you stay, he changes his
    tune:
"You are brave and beautiful.
You deserve me," he says.

We should get together.
No longer you, no longer me,
the two of us become as one.
When we become one,
the eye that sees double
will go blind.

Conversations With God

Before I ended up in this dungeon of the world,
I was with you all the time.
How I wish I'd never fallen into
this earthly trap.

I kept telling you over and over again:
"I'm perfectly happy here.
I don't want to go anywhere.
To travel from this exaltation down to Earth
is just too difficult a journey."

You sent me anyway:
　"Go, don't be scared.
No harm will come to you.
I will always be with you."

You persuaded me by saying:
"If you go, you'll gain new experiences.
You'll progress on your path.
You'll be far more mature
when you come back home."

I replied: "O Essence of Knowledge,
What good is all this learning and information
　　without you?

Who could leave you for knowledge,
unless he has no knowledge of you?"

When I drink wine from your hand,
I haven't a care in the world.
I become drunk and happy.
I couldn't care less about gain or loss,
or people's good or bad features.

The Sultan whispered a few words into my ear.
They were like the words of bandits
and left me feeling confused and out of control.

This is a long story about his deceptions.
If he really wants to do me a favor,
let an early dawn end this dark night.

The Greatness of Absence

Since seeing his face,
I can't look at other people.
One glance from him and I become drunk.

I've turned my body into wax
to receive the seal of Solomon.
In order to soften the wax,
I rub and knead it with my hands.

I threw away my false measures
after seeing him.
I became his flute and started crying when his
    lips touched me.

I was blindly searching for his hand
while all the while he was holding mine.
I was asking about him from people
who knew nothing about him.

I was so naive.
My heart was empty.
I behaved like a drunken idiot,
stealing my own gold with my own hands.

Like a thief I slipped into my garden
through a crack in the wall.
I stole roses and jasmine from my own garden.

Enough. Don't point out my secret
with your finger.
I've already suffered so much at your hands.

He knows me inside and out, hair by hair,
all my rights and wrongs.
He sees everything I do.
I can't keep anything a secret from him.

He is not the kind of sultan
who is so fond of fame and poetry
that I could impress him with verses
and long poems.

The greatness of absence is far greater
Than the illusions and promises of paradise.

Shams of Tabriz is his chosen one, his beloved.
Maybe I can impress him
with that master of the time.

How Happy a Time

How happy a time it is
when we sit on the porch,
two bodies, two forms,
but our souls as one.

When I'm with you in the garden,
our joy mixes with the birds' songs.
Stars come out to watch us.
We show our moon faces back to them.

Let's not pay attention
to any confusing superstitions.
Let's just sit down together with joy,
no you, no me.

When we start laughing,
the parrots in the sky start chewing sugar!

Even more amazing:
We are here in this corner,
and yet at the same time, you and I
are in Iraq and in Horasan.

In these forms, we are in the world.
At the same time
we are in paradise.

What a Bird!

Your kindness
keeps sending forth
favors and offers,
secretly,
without anyone knowing.

Then suddenly,
the egg hatches.
The bird of meaning flies away,
and what a bird it is!
Even the phoenix would expect good luck
from its shadow.

O Husanmeddin,
you write and praise him,
in spite of all our sorrows,
adding beauty marks
to the face of happiness.

The end of the rope
may have slipped from your hand,
but don't worry.
Shamseddin's hands would put
anklets on your feet.

Love Letter to Shams

O beloved,
our union lasted only a moment,
but our separation can be counted in years.

I watched in stunned silence
as you loaded your camel.
Suddenly night came,
and pitch darkness overwhelmed me
as I was separated from your sun-face.

You were going.
I stood frozen, in shock.
All the good times we had
were passing away.

If I hadn't been so confused in that moment,
the blood would have rushed to my face
and a howl burst from my throat.

I would have begged your pity.
I would have sacrificed my life
hundreds of times over to you,
never mind my belongings.

I would have screamed like fire
in the dark night.

The fears of the day of resurrection
would have been unleashed.

Had I done that, my heart wouldn't have had to
    go through
the tortures of separation.
It wouldn't have ended up in a situation
that causes even stones to cry.

Separation bends the straight arrow
of the back into a bow.
Tears become bloody;
the heart, naked and exposed.

O my master Shamseddin,
don't break my hope
for the sake of your soul
that is already pure
as moonlight.

Your words, those pearls of oceans deep,
turn stones into rubies
and give ecstasy to everyone.

Death Is Life for You

Separation threatened my life
and was planning to kill me.

Time opened the eye of fate at last,
but saw only my empty shell
standing in front of your door.

Love never hesitates to draw blood.
Love has neither friends nor children.

But death is life for you.
Poverty and absence are
wealth and abundance for you.

More Than These

Cupbearer, once again fill up
that glass of wine.
There's no friend like you,
either in this world
or the other.

Doing anything
but gazing at your face
is a sin against religion,
done in ignorance of the truth.

Since you showed me your face,
snatched my mind and my faith,
everywhere else has become a gallows
for the soul's Mansour.*

My soul has become crazy,
insane, because of you.
My heart has become the ocean.
How could it turn
and look at another beloved?

The vault of heaven loses all its desire
when it looks upon the Baghdad of your face,
and the beauty that surrounds you.

———
*A Sufi martyr

The glass of soul starts turning on its axis
at the tavern of lovers.
There are no drunks like them in the whole world!

Once you ride your horse farther
and advance along this road,
you will see and understand that
there are more vineyards than these,
more rose gardens than these.

What Can I Do?

My sweet-lipped beloved
never talks harshly
and never stops serving wine.

He undresses me every morning.
"Come on," he says.
"I am the one who changes your clothing."

He comes home suddenly
and doesn't give me enough time.
Whatever I do
is not enough for him.
What can I do?

I'm stunned by his glass.
After seeing him,
my body turned to soul.

Seven layers of the sky
can't contain him.
Yet he keeps moving inside of my shirt.

"You are in my hand," he says.
"I created you.
Why shouldn't I break you?"

I am your harp.
You strike your plectrum
on every part of my body.
How can't I cry?

In short,
"You can't take your heart from me,"
he says.
My heart is not my own anymore.
What can I do?

Give Up Yourself

I have seen the arrow of your glance.
"What a glory!" said my soul.
I am stretched like a bow with your pull.

I was worthless,
hidden away in the land of nowhere.
Your love came to my grave and told me,
"Get up! Jump!"

I woke up, raised by your voice.
I settled down and do as you command.
Just take care of me, O Sultan.
Offer me wine.

Give up yourself. Sit in front of me.
Make me also give up myself
so that I no longer see things as
large or small.

I am a pawn on a chessboard.
I don't need a horse to ride.
I am checkmated by you.
Put your cheek next to mine.

Serve the wine that makes the heart
like a mirror.
Don't put it off until Saturday,
not even until Thursday.

I Keep Smiling

The Earth that sinks into grief
thanks the skies and the stars:
"I shine and sparkle because of their orbits
and their lights," Earth says.

The sky thanks the sultan
for his splendor:
"It is only because of his gift that I become illuminated
and can illuminate others," sky says.

The divine sage acknowledges the gift he has
    received:
"I rose above everyone.
I became the shining star above
the seven layers of sky," sage says.

I was Venus, but became the moon,
and then the sky for hundreds of moons.
I was Joseph, and then became the One who
    creates Josephs.

O moon, I have become famous
because of you.
Look at me; then look at yourself.
Your smile turned me into a rose garden.
I keep smiling.

Why Are You Deceiving Me?

Why are you deceiving me again, O beauty?
Why are you cheating me?

I've been so kind to you.
I call you my friend.
Why are you deceiving me?

You are like life and existence itself.
Neither one has an ounce of loyalty.
How come you tell me, "You are so loyal,"
and then you go and deceive me?

My heart won't be filled
even if it drinks the river of Ceyhun.*
Why do you send me such a small water jug?

My eyes will go blind
without your moon face to gaze upon.
What can I do with a staff that
is supposed to guide me?

Why are you deceiving
the one you pardoned yesterday
with hope and fear today?

---

*The Amu Derya River, or Oxus River in Central Asia.

"One has to accept divine judgment,"
you said yesterday.
How come you're deceiving us
with words of faith and destiny today?

Since there is no cure for my ailment,
what are all these panaceas?

Eating alone has always been your custom.
Why are you inviting us to your table today?

Since you already broke the harp of joy,
How can you satisfy us
with a three-stringed instrument?

Why are you cheating us without us?
Why are you deceiving us with us?

O beautiful, in whose temple my soul
has worn the belt of service,
why are you sending us
these heavy garments?

Be silent.
All I want is you.
Why are you deceiving us
with gifts?

He Embraced Me Like His Own Soul

My beloved caressed me yesterday
and let me,
who has tasted nothing but sorrow,
taste his soul.

He gave wisdom to my mind
and put an earring in my ear.
He gave light to my eyes
and brought sweetness to my taste.

He spoke to me:
"O one who's become wasted
because of me,
O one who is afraid of me,
know that I'm kind.
I would never sell a slave I've bought."

Look and see
how he does help,
the differences he makes.
Joseph remembers the ones
who cut off their hands for him.

He embraced me like his own soul.
My doubts and ill feelings left me.
He put his beautiful face on my shoulder.

The Placeless Place

If I abandon everything in a single moment,
then I reach you.
O light-hearted beauty of the world,
offer me that heavy cup.

Offer it,
and then I'll be saved from sorrow and
    helplessness both.
I'm so tired of feeling oppressed by anxiety
and all of anxiety's other troubles.

Offer it to me,
for then I'll be drunk with God's glass
and be annihilated completely.
I'll open my wings in absence
and fly away to the placeless place.

Everyone Else Is a Stranger

God served me wine,
like rain pouring from a cloud,
and got me drunk.
The cupbearer has immersed me
in his flowing favors.

O wine that lifts me up
and relieves my anxieties,
I came here only so
you could reveal my secrets.

Love has inflicted so many pains on me.
But that's how my life became blessed.

Offer, O cupbearer,
offer up the rest of the wine.
You don't have to beckon me.
I'm already yours, O my faithless friend.

He's everywhere around us.
Our eyes are wide open to him.
We wear dresses made of his light.
Our elegance won't fade away.

O my ear, my candle,
O my drunkenness, my gratitude,
O my wine and my soul,
everyone else beside you is a stranger to me.

Beautiful One

Glory and majesty are in your hands,
O beautiful one.
We are your helpless prey.
You are the lion hunter,
O beautiful.

O our peace bringing beauty,
the light and candle of our hearts.
Both worlds and houses
are under your control,
O beautiful.

Every single particle
prostrates before your door.
Everyone is your slave as well as your friend.
How sweet you are, O beloved,
O beautiful.

With every breath
I become thirstier and hungrier for you.
I have the hunger of an ox!
"Could you drink the ocean?" you asked.
"Yes! I could to the very last drop,
O beautiful!"

I swear to God that
anyone who stays with you never dies.
If there is such a thing as death,
I hope it finds me at your temple,
O beautiful.

I don't have a shop, and I earn no profit.
I'm a vagrant in this world.
I don't know how anyone accomplishes
anything but you,
O beautiful.

I don't know if it's still night or if the dawn has come.
What is awareness anyway?
Only you can count the days,
O beautiful.

Seeing you is the pleasure of my day.
Separating from you is the sorrow of my night.
Because of you, my night turns into day,
O beautiful. You are the day.

You are my garden, full of blessings.
You are my resplendent rose sapling.
No one has ever seen such a springtime as you,
O beautiful, and such a thing will never be seen.

You turn my body to dust,
then purify my dust and resurrect me.
You are my moonfaced beauty,
O beautiful.

The philosopher becomes blind.
His eyesight leaves him.
He can't see the hyacinth of faith
you plant in front of him.

The philosopher is my self.
The one who understands you
is my drunkenness and ecstasy.
Don't pay attention to ordinary beauty,
or to other people's flaws.
You are my peerless beauty,
O beautiful one.

The Promise Is Sweet

O one whose blessings
cannot be counted in numbers.
No one can refuse
to serve you.

You created us
as noble creatures so that
we could worship you.
How wonderful you are!

You're beyond needing
our praise and thanks.
But by praising you, we praise ourselves,
and that's the reason you want us to praise
and thank you.

Your grace and kindness
brought us the good news,
the promise that we would meet.

The promise of the beautiful is sweet.
Happiness comes only from you
and snatches hundreds of hearts in a single breath.

Still Say Nothing

Yesterday I went completely crazy.
Love saw me:
"Don't wail. Don't tear your clothing.
I've come," he said.

"O love," I cried out, "I'm not afraid of
      anything,"
"But nothing exists," he said.
"So don't even talk about it.

"I'll whisper a secret in your ear.
Just answer me by shaking your head.
But don't talk.

"A moonlike soul
Has appeared on the way to the heart.
The journey to the heart is so gratifying.
But don't say anything about it to anyone."

This time, I asked the heart:
"O heart, what kind of moon is that?"
He called back to me:
"This is not something that you can understand
      with your mind.
So don't say a word."

I persisted, "Is this something angelic or human?"
"Neither," he answered.
"Shhhh. Don't talk."

I said, "I've just about passed out of myself.
I feel turned completely upside down."
"Be like that," he said.
"Just don't talk.

"O one who stays in a house
cluttered with shapes and images,
pack your belongings,
and get out of this place.
But don't say a word."

"O heart," I begged, "Please treat me like you're
      my father.
Isn't that one of God's attributes?"
"Yes," he said, "Of course it is.
But even then, O soul of your father,
Still say nothing."

Flying High On Your Wine

Cupbearer, stain us with the color of your wine.
Take us beyond ourselves, so much so that
both worlds will disappear from our perception.

Keep offering us bottle after bottle of wine so that
our load will get ever lighter.
Your wine will make us fly!

Place our soul on the back of red wine's horse,
and send us galloping toward love.
Two hundred miles will be but a step for us.

Cupbearer, walk as fast as you can.
Thoughts are like large boulders in the road.
They're such a bother, and they hurt our soul.
Please remove them.

Offer Your Wine

Beloved, offer us wine in the early evening.
You are the light of our eyes.

Every morning we take our share
from your hand.
O sun-faced, turn the glasses over.

Offer it to me alone,
not to others.
Keep your word.
You are the loyal sultan.
You are the moon.

As a new moon,
you appear from behind the veils of dust.
You are the remedy for all our troubles.

Turn the glass.
Now is the time for your love.

With all your glory, my sultan,
kindly be my cupbearer.
We are your thirsty drunks.

Please Don't Go

It doesn't matter if the eye, the mind,
and the soul should all get up and leave.
Let them go.
But don't you ever go away.
Seeing you here
is better than having all of them.

The sun and the sky took shelter in your shadow.
Even the sky and the stars depart.
Don't go.

O one whose most garbled words
are purer than essence,
let the essence go.
But don't you go.

The faithful are afraid of being separated from
their faith in their last few breaths.
My only fear is to be separated from you.
Don't go.

Don't go.
But if you must, then take my soul with you.

It Wasn't Like That

My beloved's face and cheeks
weren't like that.
The leaves and fruits of the trees in my garden
weren't like that.

People everywhere
are changing their minds.
This wasn't the custom of this place before.

Why has the soul fallen
into this deep, dark cave?
The promised help of the friend of the cave*
wasn't like that.

So many torrents of sorrows
washed away my load and my donkey.
This wasn't what I expected
from my dear friend with whom I shared my troubles.

What kind of meal is the beloved cooking up for me?
That wasn't what the master promised.

———
*Ebu Bakr, the first Caliph who spent the night with the Prophet
in a cave.

He hid the trap,
put the bait in front of me
and concealed his intentions.
This is not what he said he would do.

The one who advised me
gave me the wrong advice
and made me lose my way.
He was supposed to be trustworthy,
but he wasn't.

Moaning and weeping grew like thorns
in the lawn of joy and pleasure.
That famed spring wouldn't let that happen.

Your burglar became a guard
who tied my hands.
This isn't the way of justice or protection
promised by the sultan.

You didn't give me a chance
to give you my excuse.
I didn't expect this from the one
who is solid as a mountain.

Your harsh words have the smell of blood about
    them,
not the smell of musk
from the belly button of the gazelle.

What kind of wind is this samiel?*
All the leaves are fallen.
This isn't what you told me
when we sat together under the tree.

I've become exhausted with remorse
over a small guilt.
This isn't how
the great ones should act.

What is this business?
What is this torment?
I never thought my moment of reckoning
would look like this.

This isn't my way
nor these events mine.
That sweetly drunk camel
wasn't this camel.

I should go to the sultan
and complain about the cheatings of this swindler.
It wasn't my gold that was counterfeit.

The sultan is like the sea.
His treasure box is filled with pearls,
but his treasure looks nothing like this one.

———
*A desert breeze that brings disasters.

Enough.
I'm just whining.
The prey of my sultan
who prays and is praised
is not that one.

Shamseddin

If you are a true seeker
of the secret of the heart,
Shamseddin, greatest of the greats,
will become your beloved.

Once you fall into the seas
of Shamseddin,
the lights of the whole world
will appear to you.

Just like God,
you will rip and tear down
and, at the same time,
sew and repair.
You will open and close,
both at the same time.

If you want,
you can appear
or conceal yourself,
however you like.

You will see everyone, everything,
bare and naked,
yet no one can see you.

In the land of soul,
you will be the sultan of sultans,
and you will be given
your own, special cave.

Shamseddin will become your pride and joy.
You will turn into a servant
at the door of the cave.

Keep saying,
Shamseddin, Shamseddin.
Cry out from Shamseddin to Shamseddin.

But if he doesn't want you to,
you'll never find him.

The Road Is Narrow

That tough, belligerent Turk
came to make peace
and hold my hand.
"May God be our judge," he said.

I asked about fate,
its awkward turns.
He bit his lips as if to say,
"Quit talking this nonsense."

"Why does it turn like that?" I asked.
"Wet wood," he said, "always smokes.
Smoke gives a headache."

"Have you heard anything new?" I asked.
"New news can't get in an old ear," he said.

Tell me if you know the secret of
my small, slanting-eyed Turk.

My vision is not feeble,
but the road is narrow.
Open the road from my narcissus eyes
to his place.

Don't Go Away

Don't shake your head like that, my sultan.
Don't put on your turban.
Don't go.
O moon, whose eyes and face are so beautiful.
Don't go away.

Who in this world
has clear eyes and a pure heart?
Don't die.
Don't hurt me.
Don't run off to strangers.

Don't leave the friend,
and don't burn our house of secrets to the ground.
Don't leave the rose garden
and run after every thorn.

My friend, don't be so stubborn,
and don't try to deceive me.
Don't get belligerent.
You know you left that time.
Don't do it again.

I am your slave and servant.
You trained me and changed me.
O heart, don't go away.

I am your flute,
drunk on your melodies.
Don't break the harp of joy.
Don't break the string.
Don't go away.

If you're drunk already,
why go elsewhere?
Sit next to the jar.
Don't leave the cupbearer who serves you.
Don't go away.

O one who gives your life like an alm,
who gives your soul away so freely,
nothing is better than this.
Don't go away. Don't do anything else.

Don't get lost in thoughts and dreams.
Don't turn away from what's real
and run after traces.
Don't turn your face from the beloved.

O beauty of soul,
Be coy. Bite your tongue. Tighten your jaw.
Don't go away.

You are the archangel of kindness.
The lotus tree is your home and country.

Don't fly away to the mountains and forests
like the birds of this world.

You know perfectly well
that no soul can come back to life without you.
Open the door to your blessings.
Don't stay hidden behind it.

Listen to the rest of the poem
from the sultan of sultans.
Just listen.
Don't bother with the words.

Lifting the Curtain

You're a lion.
We're just empty saddlebags.
What's a saddlebag compared to a lion?

Lift the curtain in front of our eyes.
Lift, so that Satan will go blind.

So many people became drunk
In front of the beloved's face.
What is bread?
They have no idea.

His Trace

O interested listeners,
hear the story of the chief of police.
A rind* has run away
from our neighborhood circle.

We felt burned and ruined,
kept looking for him everywhere.
Day and night, we searched high and low.

Then, someone in the neighborhood
found his trace.
Come and see.
These are his bloody clothes.

In fact, the blood of lovers never dries.
It always stays fresh.
If the blood is new,
it is easy to find to whom it belongs.

All blood gets old,
becomes dark and dries up,
except for the blood of lovers.
It keeps flowing from the heart
and remains fresh to the end.

———————
*An unconventional, humorous sage.

Don't dismiss this story by saying,
"Who cares? This is just an old blood feud."
The blood of lovers has never slept in this world
and never will.

Only your bloody eyes shed blood in this town.
Your narcissus eyes used to be the cupbearer.
You served big glasses all around.
Your glance comes as a drunkard
and steals hearts.

Do me a favor: Either give me back
what's been lost
or come forward
and admit that it's gone.

Be grateful, O heart.
When you receive a favor from the master of sugar,
dissolve like sugar into sugar.

If you are killed like that,
you become immortal.
Send greetings to Tabriz
from the soul of one
who died like that.*

————
*In this poem, Rumi begins to accept that Shams has been
assassinated.

Wherever You Are

I was buried and rotting
in the grave of myself.
When you came to visit me,
I raised my head and
climbed out of my tomb.

You are the trumpet
that is blown on my last day of judgment.
What can I do? Dead or alive,
wherever you are, I am there.

I am like a lifeless piece of reed,
ever silent when your lips are not around.
But if you play me like a ney,*
your breath turns me into divine melodies.

I bind my head if I can't see you.
I bite my hands if I can't find your sweet lips.

---

*A reed flute.

Don't Go Anywhere Without Me

Don't throw stones
at the glassmaker's counter.
Don't hurt the one
whose heart is already broken.

Throw all those stones at me instead.
As long as I'm standing here,
it's a pity to waste your stone
and hit someone else.

Set free all of sorrow's captives
but me.
When you need to torture someone,
don't turn your eyes from me.

Either you like me or you don't.
It's all okay.
Just don't go anywhere without me.

Your Blessing Is Unconditional

No one can steal the dice
from the Earth's pocket.
So don't even try.
You won't be able to get them out.

I'll take the pearl of faith
instead of the dice.
If you're hesitant to give your soul,
you won't be able to return it
to the beloved.

O God's captivating love,
your kindness never ceases.
You'll never abandon the people
until you give them what they desire.

Grab hold of our skirt and pull us nicely over
    to yourself.
You never lead the heart in the wrong direction.
You always keep your word, never giving up,
pulling everyone merrily along to your place.

You set hundreds of requirements,
but your blessing is unconditional.

You are not greedy.
You don't put the gold in your pocket.

Don't say a thing.
My tongue and lips, don't talk.
You can't be Bedeshan's* ruby
if you hang around a stone-hearted one.

---

*Bedeshan was a city famous for its rubies.

Songs of Advice, Songs of Admonition

*I*magine the small and winding streets of a thirteenth-century Turkish town. Imagine Rumi as an ecstatic drunkard wandering around town, calling out to everybody he passes as he dances and staggers through the streets. On one corner are the lovers, and he stops and speaks to them softly, encouraging them to keep surrendering to this mystery that has taken hold of them. On the next corner are the people who revere him and his great friend Shams. Rumi acknowledges them for the wisdom of their vision and their continued commitment to enter into the heresy themselves. A few blocks later, he comes across the naysayers, the scowling faces of disapproval, the ones who behind everyone's backs are plotting for the downfall of both Rumi and Shams. Rumi does not shy away from meeting their disapproval with disapproving words of his own.

Like a physician of the soul who liberally distributes medicines to the ill, Rumi dispenses advice on every street corner. Take this, he says, take it diligently, take it for the rest of your life, and watch what happens to you. Watch your illness drop away, like some concealing curtain, and then see what vistas of your soul are revealed.

We all suffer from the illness of the soul, and our symptoms are remarkably similar. We listen to the chatter in our minds as though it were God himself speaking. We are swept this way and that by our fluctuating emotions, desires, and fancies, as though the tides of the ocean itself were sweeping through our bodies. Everywhere we look, we get confirmation of our separation from the world outside of ourselves. The more we come to know about the vastness of that world, the more we feel small, alone, alienated, fearful of the discrepancy in size between our little body and the very large world.

But, Rumi tells us, there's a cure to this illness, a solution to this insoluble dilemma. The consciousness of union, in which the soul experiences its inherent connection and oneness with everything that is, is every bit as real and palpable as is the far more common consciousness of separation. The antidote to the fear of separation is to be found through dissolving into union, and guess what? The medicines to effect this cure have already been ingested. In fact, they have been inside you from the moment you were born, waiting patiently on the shelves for you to have the good sense to take them down, swallow them whole, and let the healing begin.

The medicines Rumi dispenses are both sweet and bitter. For those clearly on the path of the heart, the words are a comfort to the soul. But for those who stand in opposition to the ways in which the divine energies want to pass through them, the unminced words may be difficult to hear. Rumi is not afraid to respond to the fiery words of those who doubt him with fire of his own. For him there can be no compromises to the divine truth that all of us are children of God and that our birthright is to inherit the inner riches of that kingdom.

If you want to ignite the heretic's transformation of consciousness, you need to let go of ingrained habits and behaviors that no longer serve you, and embrace new ones that do. Rumi tells us how to do this.

Search There

Sometimes you get as frightened
as a camel.
Sometimes you get stuck in the mud
like hunted prey.

O young fool,
how long will you keep running away from
    yourself?
In the end,
the thing will happen anyway.

Just go in the direction
where there is no direction.
Go, search there.

The Best Nourishment

Life on Earth has its ups and downs.
Sometimes it's pleasant; sometimes not.
You'd better fall in love with someone
who will make you the immortal sultan.

Since everyone's life is black and white,
search for another life
made from the radiance of God's light.

O one who has gotten lost in himself,
you're not aware that your life has become a grave.
In fact, you are buried in the grave of yourself.

Finding the one who gave you life
is the best nourishment for you.
Yet you are running like fire from one store
to the other
for the food that can be measured
in cups.

Fasting

The kitchen of the body darkens
the lives of lovers.
Fasting came to enlighten them.

Fasting is an amazing thing.
It gives people heart and soul.

If you want to ascend like the Prophet to the sky
of immortality,
know this very well:
Fasting is your Arabian stallion.

Fasting blinds the body
in order to open the eyes of your soul.
Faith alone can't provide illumination
when the eyes of your heart are blind.

Divine Road

A shepherd comes every night
from the land of absence,
frees souls from the bodies
and scatters them like camels.

He guides them secretly
back to the land of absence
and places them lovingly
in the pasture of his kindness.

But he covers their eyes
and doesn't let them see the road,
for this is a divine road,
not the road of self and senses.

Choose Love

Because of the beloved
my heart is happy,
my soul illuminated.

From the beloved's greenery
hundreds of blessed rivers
are flowing to the rose gardens.

In order to enter into your rose garden,
the souls make peace with the thorns.

Choose love. Choose love.
Without this beautiful love,
life is nothing but a burden.

God's Ocean

The soul of the universe is a pure and clean ocean.
Forms and shapes are the foams on that sea.
Plunge into this pure, clean ocean.
Don't just play with the foams.

The foams on the sea's surface never stand still.
Waves constantly move them about.
When they dry up, they're no longer even part of
    the sea.

The foam either turns into water
or becomes part of the sand,
because two colors cannot fit
into God's one ocean.

The wave comes from the sea,
then watches and bows down to itself.
"O, Ocean, essence of my existence," wave says,
"How did you turn into so many waves?"

All souls are one.
All existence is but the reflection of the Sultan.

Watch How God Opens the Door

I'm grateful for whatever God gives me.
All my labor and efforts are dedicated to him.

Whatever you've done in the past,
I pray God gives you his blessing
and I pray that he will bless you for the future as
 well.

Free the soul and the heart
from the thoughts of the mind.
You're the only one who can do that.

If soul and heart were content with reason,
why do they run to music
and search for ecstasy?

Since God wants you to be pure and clean,
O heart, you'll just look stupid
if you try to act smart.

You keep on devouring yourself
like a dung beetle in the mud.
You might as well stay there. It's what you
 deserve.

Know this well:
Everyone, including the sultan,
is in deep trouble.
Love hits everybody.

Be silent. Watch how God opens the door.
Why are you lost in the thought
that closes the door?

The Journey Starts Here

Don't go off sightseeing.
The real journey is right here.
The great excursion starts from exactly where
   you are.
You are the world.
You have everything you need.
You are the secret.
You are the wide opened.

Don't look for the remedy for your troubles
outside yourself.
You are the medicine.
You are the cure for your own sorrow.

Ascend the Mountain of Love

Don't lose your way by becoming a nonconformist.
Don't get caught up in anything else either.
Come walk with me instead.
Together we will ascend the mountain of love.

Don't let the distance we must walk bother you.
When we reach our destination, there'll be a
wedding celebration,
and Union will embrace you.

The wind of joy and pleasure blows
at the very beginning of this road.
It gives strength and sustenance
to the travelers.

Don't You Recall?

Do you know where you came from?
You came from God's harem, that's where.
Yes, from God, who is without fault or defect.

Try to remember. Don't you recall
those divine, beautiful lips?

In truth, you've forgotten them,
and that's why you're so confused
and your head is spinning.

You've been selling your soul for a handful of dirt.
What a lousy deal!

Return that dirt. Know your value.
You aren't a slave. You're the master.
You're the sultan.

Beautiful faces came down secretly from the sky,
just for you.

These Two Worlds

Our joy and pleasure
are beyond imagining.
For us, a smile is a veil.

O cross-eyed villagers,
these two worlds are double for you,
but only one for us.

O man of longing,
we've put a guide for you
at every crossroad.

Be silent.
Don't look for fame.
Ride your horse
into the soul's rose garden instead.
I have a rose there waiting for you.

Outside the Sack

What's happened to the newlyweds?
What shape are they in now?
If you understand this,
you won't have to participate in this world's games.

The world put hundreds of thousands
of intellectuals into the sack.
Where is the truly intelligent one
who's managed to stay outside the sack?

A Rascal in the Bazaar

There's a rascal in the bazaar,
a real slippery character, as wily as they come.
He's an insufferable windbag
and will say anything to get what he wants.

He's in hot water with the inspector
as well as with the supervisor of the bazaar.
From the pharmacist to the boza* maker,
everyone's complaining about him.

When they say to him,
"Why are you destroying the bazaar?
Don't touch anything! Hold your tongue! Shame
    on you,"
he becomes contrite and promises a hundred
    times,
"I won't do it again. I won't touch a thing.
I'll stay far away."

Then he goes and steals from his neighbors
and pawns their valuables.
He uses the money
to buy wine and throws parties.

----

*A drink made of fermented millet.

Then he acts like he's deathly ill
and throws himself to the ground trembling.
When you see him, you think he's had malaria
    for years.

But it's all fake.
He does this only to make others feel sorry for him.

He tells everyone who will listen to him,
"At such-and-such a place, with so-and-so
I've got so much gold and silver.
To whomever helps me with my sickness,
I'll return the favor a hundred times over."

He shaves many people's heads* this way,
taking their money and swindling them.

When they realize they've been fleeced,
they throw dirt on their heads and rip their
    collars,
all because of this cruel rascal.

His tongue is a hundred yards long
and looks so sweet.
But when you see the wounds he opens,
his mouth is just a deep pit filled with snakes.

———

*Cheats people.

If you try to kick him out,
he starts talking and tells the funniest jokes.
His words are as sweet as honey.

He becomes so full of love and kindness.
Dropping to the floor in front of you,
he makes you fall in love with him.
Your heart bursts open, and you forget all your
    upsets.

To hear him brag about his goodness and his talents
you'd think he's the Lokman* of our time.

When he talks about devoutness,
he shaves your head as smooth as a pumpkin or a
    cucumber.

The time comes, and he starts talking about
absence and God's knowledge,
impressing us so much, we can only exclaim,
"He's either Cuneyd† or some other great sheikh!"

But if you dig a little deeper, if you search,
you'll see it's all deception and treachery.

---

*Lokman: A legendary Sufi.

†Cuneyd Baghdadi: A great Sufi (d. 910).

He's a disaster really, total garbage.
He doesn't care about anyone but himself.

He doesn't have a real job or even an occupation.
He's just greedy, that's all.
He goes from table to table, stuffing himself.

He's as crooked as they come.
Even the best bazaar inspector
is bamboozled by his tricks.

When he cries and wails,
everyone, big and small, comes rushing to his aid
even though they know he doesn't need it.

The inspector is your mind,
the bazaar your disposition.
And that dirty, deceitful rascal in the bazaar
is your self.

Everybody's exasperated with him.
They've all lost their shirts.
They say this rascal casts a spell on everyone.

Since he's a gifted sorcerer, it's difficult to deal
  with him.
The only thing we can profitably do

is stay far away from him.
Go instead to the place of the greatest of greats.

We should take shelter there with our
sultan Shamseddin.
He has eyes in his head as well as in his soul.
The soul's face turned into hundreds of beauties
because of him.

We should tell him about this rascal's treachery
and ask his help.
He could save us all from so much misery
in a single moment.

If the giants and djinns knew of his majesty,
they'd become the great devotees of the time.
No one can be freed from the darkness of that
   terrible self
until they accept his help, like a breeze in
   springtime.

The earth of Tabriz turned into the sacred land
   of Kaabe because of him.
The blessing that visitors get from him
is enough for anyone.

Just Do It

Who can find a trace of you?
There isn't even a bit of dust from your track.
Who could find your home?
You have no home.

How can I praise you?
What can I say about you?
Foam is the only form in the sea of meaning.

A great, unseen town
lies just behind that curtain.
Our world is nothing compared to that.

Don't lower yourself.
Don't knock on every door.
You yourself are what you're looking for.

O heart, raise your tent up to the sky.
Don't say, "I can't."
Sure you can. Just do it.

Your Overflowing Secrets

Never mind what the world does.
What do you do?
Worlds always become houses of idols.
Where is your hidden beauty?

Let's suppose that famine covered the earth.
From now on, nothing—no bread, no soup, no
    food on the table.
O one who sometimes reveals himself
and sometimes remains hidden,
where is your pantry, where is your granary?

Let's suppose that the world became a field of thorns,
filled with snakes and scorpions.
O soul's musician, O joy of the soul,
where is your rose garden?

Let's suppose that generosity died,
that greed killed everyone.
O our heart, where is your kindness,
where is your gifting?

Let's suppose the moon and sun have gone away,
become invisible.
O one who shows us how to see and hear,
where is your blaze? Where is your light?

Let's suppose no merchant was left to sell pearls.
How come you're not decked out in jewels?
Where are your clouds that rain pearls?

Let's suppose that not a single mouth or tongue
could be found to reveal a secret.
Alright, but . . . how can you hide your
   overflowing secrets?

The Drunks of Union

Come to your senses!
We're the drunks of Union!
It's getting late, come earlier next time.
Where did you say your tavern was?

Look carefully at our drunk,
if you're not confused or senile.
Ask him: Where is your robe?
Where's your turban?

One son of a bitch grabbed your turban,
the other pinched your robe, that's where!
Your face is paler than the moon.
Where's your protector?
Who's taking care of you?

A stranger came and started harassing the
      eternal drunks.
Why aren't you racing to their aid?
Where's your courage?
Where's your bravery?

O one who scatters words,
be silent, be like the listening ear instead.
Don't be just a wordsmith to the people.
Where is your ecstasy?
Where are your words about ecstasy?

Ahead of the Thought

If a thought comes into your mind,
think also its opposite, for either one may come true.

Hesitation between two ideas may confuse you.
Opposing views may lead you to the truth.

See the end of the road while you are still
ahead of the thought.
How long will you waste time with words?

The Land of Absence

The wandering mind came yesterday and
  knocked on my door.
"Who's there?" I asked. "Open the door, and
  come on in."

"How can I come in?" he answered. "Your house
  is on fire.
Absence burns everything with his fire."

"Don't worry, " I said to him. "Be brave, come in.
He cleans you of your self,
and when he chooses you,
it's all over. You're finished."

There's a universe called Absence.
Its waves break on the shore of existence.
Jump right into that wave,
and if anyone asks, just say you're a Sufi.
A Sufi doesn't give a thought to his past.

You'll see your candle light up all the other candles,
and its light will mix with the light of all the
  great luminaries.

The wave of that sea carries you
to just such a place in the land of Absence.

There it breaks the ties of your soul
from everything you're attached to.

Only in the land of Absence can you discover
    your Absolute Being.
You'll become the king at the harem of Absence.
Everyone will follow you there.

Existence itself won't be able to look at you
because the light of your greatness would blind
    its eyes.

Love Is Its Own Proof

How long will you keep on crying,
"Where's my remedy?
Where's my cure?"
Whoever it is that's making you search for a remedy,
go look for him.

How long will you stay mired in sadness, complaining,
"Sorrow has taken my soul away"?
What is the soul?
Why don't you try to find it?

Did you smell a loaf of bread?
Go toward that smell.
That smell will tell you everything you need to
    know about bread.

If you fall in love,
your love is your proof
and that's enough.
If you're not in love,
what good is proof?

Advice to the Drunk at Heart

Just as the feet always find their shoes in the dark,
so the heart finds its place through pleasure.

Get inside the heart.
Board Noah's Ark in that flood.
There may be fear in the air,
but don't put it in your heart.

Be afraid of your desire and its fancies,
but never of actual events.

Don't do things to others
if you don't want them done to you.

Put cotton in your ears.
Don't listen to every word that's spoken.
You may have a clean soul,
but even a clean soul can gather rust.

If you want to attain,
hang around the attained ones.
You can't ask for Union from one who's not
    already unified.

Live among the drunks.
Even if there's not much wine,

the smell will be enough.
The sober one only knows the table on which
   the wine sits.

If you feel your faults don't allow you to mature,
then be with Shams-i Tabriz.
Let his maturity mature you.

Light and Shadow

O Candle of the World,
your light was absent from our circle last night.
Tell me the truth:
Where was the light of your cheek?

Look at my heart.
It has been destroyed by the desire
to see your face.
May you live
long and longer!

All last night until early dawn
I paced back and forth, crying.
Morning came, and still
my eyes were open.

You are the shadow of divine light.
We are your shadow in this world.
Who has ever seen a shadow
separated from the light?

Sometimes the shadow stays
next to the light.
Sometimes it disappears into the light.
If it is next to the light,
light and shadow are equal to each other.

When it disappears, it merges
and unites with the light.

When it realizes it's disappearing,
The shadow grabs the light tightly
with the hand of desire.
In order to have God's radiance,
this desire takes him to God.

The story of the union and separation
of light and shadow never ends.

Light is the creator of every reason
that exists in his shadows.
God made "no reason" as
the ultimate reason for everything.

Words into Dust

The brilliance of his peerless words
leaves the sages feeling embarrassed.

Every particle in the sands of the desert,
if it only gets his scent,
becomes the bird of life,
opens its wings,
and flies away.

When they fly,
they don't bother with words.
They turn them back into dust at your tent,
bewildered and dispersed.

Time to Journey

Night has come,
time for solitude and privacy.
Lovers turn their faces to the moon.

O, moon worshippers,
the moon is smiling.
O, night passengers,
time to start the journey.

Sleep has come.
All "I's" and "we's" are forgotten.
This is the sleepless time
for those who accept God.

Essence is like grain
mixed up in the body's straw.
Once the body has fallen into sleep
essence stands alone.

Come as You Are

Where is Islam's accent when it comes to the
    language of love?
If you surrender yourself to your essence,
the whole world surrenders to you.

Every day spent in separation feels as long as a year.
But when you come out of separation,
Where does the day go? And what becomes of
    the night?

On this pilgrimage, removing the dress of your
    existence
is the cloak you must wear.
But who will be able to comply
with the conditions of this cloak?

Village and town, near and far, the changing
    seasons,
all are on this side of the sea.
But on the other side, where is the town?
Where are the seasons?

Man's mind and reason have created the cold
    loneliness of separation.
But when he warms up with that wine,
Where is the mind? And what becomes of reason?

A bird in the cage
is under someone else's control.
But when he breaks the cage and flies away,
what becomes of the control? Where even is the
      bird?

When the mind is confined to the head,
it tempts the body to commit sins.
But when the mind of minds explodes open,
where are the sins now? Where is the body?

If you drink,
go swaying to the land of secrets
without your feet.
If you're already drunk, then come as you are.
Where has your mind gone?
And where is the need to be something you are
      not?

The Language of the Heart

What is it with my heart
that holds itself back from becoming yours?
What is it with my body
that resists annihilation?

Let's say I own the sky and the moon.
If they don't give off light,
what use are they to me?

Let's say I go to paradise
and am bathed in blessings.
Since it torments me
not to see your face,
what good is paradise?
What good are the blessings?

Since you are the one
who scolds children for misbehaving,
How could soul and heart
stay away from making mischief?

A jasmine doesn't smile,
a tree's branch doesn't move,
a plant doesn't grow and send forth fragrance
without the morning breeze.

When you made it poor
and took away its belongings,
the moon didn't care that it had no kaftan.

How amazing that the ignorant
don't pay the heart much attention.
But everyone can't be
a master or sultan.

His kindness summons all the guilty
to his door.
But when you get there,
you're forgiven.

Let the soul be.
Never mind the moon in the sky.
I swear on the name of God
that there is nothing like God.

O soul, don't run away from
the troubles of love.
You'll just become vain without them.

Nights are so beautiful in the presence of that moon.
He is so like the moon
that all he has is face,
nothing else.

Such a sultan that acts
like a slave and a servant,
such a beloved that
never leaves the side of his friend.

Be silent, O body.
Let my heart talk.
There is neither "I" nor "we"
in the language of the heart.

Free Wine

After seeing your pure and clean water,
I understood the story of the soul.
I disappeared from sight, just like a soul.
I drowned in the waters of Nothingness.

The one who loves the smell of musk
hunts for the gazelle.
When you run after him,
he also runs after you.

To stay sober in front of God's cupbearer
is absolute blasphemy.
The soul keeps turning somersaults
because the wine is served free of charge.

O brother, it's such a relief
to be free from the self both day and night.
Become the greatest drunk of God.
You'll be second to no one.

There are so many drunks hidden in that green square,
and I'm walking right toward them.
You know that already, but I'm telling you again.

They are so beautiful,
the lights of Muhammad's lineage,
a gift from God.

The Perfect Host

If you hurry, if you run,
you'll come across the water birds.
You'll find the waters of life
and reach the sea of endless joy.

You've eaten all kinds of foods,
some sweet, others salty.
You've tasted all the pleasures of life.
Just once, come to Love.
Let him become your host.

A Helper of Hearts

Don't look down on the heart,
even if it's not behaving well.
Even in that shape, the heart
is more precious than the teachings of the
    exalted saints.

The broken heart is where God looks.
How lucky is the soul that mends this heart!

For God, consoling the heart
that is broken into hundreds of pieces
is better than going on pilgrimage.

God's treasures are buried in ruined hearts.

If you put on the belt of service
and serve hearts
like a slave or servant,
the roads to all the secrets
will open in front of your eyes.

If you want peace and glory,
forget about your earthly honors
and try to please the hearts.

If you become
a helper of hearts,
springs of wisdom
will flow from your heart.

The water of life will run from your mouth
like a torrent.
Your breath will become medicine
like the breath of Jesus.

Be silent.
Even if you have two hundred tongues
in each hair on your head,
You won't be able to explain
the heart.

A Life Without Art

A life without the love of art
Is an empty, wasted life.
Nothing else matters.
Other words are nonsense on this path.

God's Artistry

Leave your art alone.
Let the Creator be enough for you.

He is the One who makes something
out of nothing.
He is the One who changes the false
into the real.

All That Is Good

Look and see:
All that is good
comes from the heart.
All that's not good
comes from mixing water with dirt.

If you chase after your desires,
overcome by lust,
The mud around you will increase one hundred
    fold.
Salvation comes when you give up
the fancies and desires
that opened the door to all your troubles in the
    first place.

The only reason you can't give up your desires
is that you're lazy.
Since you are the problem,
it will follow you
wherever you go.

Promise yourself that
you won't break your oath.
Otherwise the disease will remain
and the cure will be lost.

If you stay firm in that oath,
Your soul will give birth to
one hundred thousand pleasures.

Then this iron heart
will turn into a mirror.
At every moment, a mature and perfect face
will look back at you.

Open the Door

Half of my body is fighting
with the other half.
Don't just stand there.
Come, do something, reconcile them.

A raven and a falcon
put in the same cage
inflict so much suffering on each other.

Open the cage so they can come back to life.
The fight ends when you open the door.

Reason and being are locked inside our chest.
They keep fighting each other.
Both are in bad shape
and feeling woozy from separation.

If you want them to fight,
close the door.
If you don't,
then be a peacemaker.

Donkey and Ox

Where is my donkey?
Where is my donkey?
My donkey died last year,
thank God.
Since then my headache has departed too.

My ox may also die.
Let it die.
I won't be sorry.
Neither the ox nor its belly
smelled like my divine ambergris.

Nothing would change
if the donkey died or the ox disappeared.
In both worlds, my beauty,
the one who caught my heart
would live forever.

My donkey used to wear a golden earring.
A donkey adorned in gold,
consider that and feel sorry.
Alas, my gold, alas.

My donkey was hardheaded,
slow on the journey,
didn't like barley,

didn't do me one bit of good except for
piling dung in front of my door.

There is an ox in the sky.*
There's another under the ground.
If I could free myself from both of them,
I would jump right over the wheel of fortune.

I went to the bazaar where they sell donkeys.
I looked all around.
My eyes and heart were filled with donkeys
and their owners.

Someone said:
"Since your donkey died,
Why don't you buy another?"
"Be quiet," I replied,
"My donkey was a handicap on this road."

---

*The image of an ox in the sky refers to the signs of the zodiac.

Checkmate

When a pedestrian puts his face
on the Sultan's feet,
He will ride away from poverty
with two horses.

After that, he can never go backward,
like the queen in chess.

Be checkmated.
Quit the game of whisper.
The chess master
is the One who could guide you.

The Caravan's Bells

Love and patience do not go together.
Reason cannot stop your tears.

Ecstasy is like a beautiful town
that cannot be controlled by any one of its
    inhabitants.

The caravan of life is passing us by,
but no one can hear the sound of the bells.

Steal Pearls

Whoever is dizzy
feels that the ones who are seated are turning.

Whoever is nearsighted
comes close to look at people's faces.
He looks so funny with his crossed eyes.

Whoever has yellow jaundice
tastes bitterness, even if he chews sugar.

The mind is like a lame donkey at his square,
But who has ever seen God's Burak* limping?

If you know how to bore a hole,
drill it through the Sultan's walls.
If you steal something from a house,
steal pearls.

---

*The name of the horse on which the Prophet ascended to heaven.

This Temporary World

You're going to be expelled
from this temporary world,
even if you sit very still.
But you don't know that,
and keep spinning in this vortex.

Try to run toward the river
of God's mercy instead.

Stamp your feet on this world of troubles
so that I can caress you
with my hands of hope.

Your hair smells better
than musk and ambergris.
You should be the one
who challenges the rose.
With such beautiful curly hair,
you should throw your hat to the sky.

How could this world
deceive someone like you,
so bright and sharp,
with just a few words?

The world talks slowly and softly,
but lashes out very hard.
You can't match this donkey!

If he confronts you with a proof
that is upside down,
throw it back in his face.

This ogre is pulling you into the desert
and wants you to spend your life there.
Argue with this ogre!

Why are you so dumbstruck?
Answer him.
His words are all wrong.

Some Advice

Come friends, good or bad,
here's some advice for you
on the long road of life.

Stay close to the shepherd.
Lots of wolves are around.
Hear this from me, my little black lamb.

Be Iranian, Greek, or Turk,
but speak the silent language of the mute.

If this side of the green stick burns,
the other end will surely cry.

Sacrifice yourself like Ishmael
for this Love,
because night sacrifices itself
to morning all the time.

Be silent.
That lion of lions shines the light of meaning
    without words
but he was reduced to a leopard
because of his roar.

Music at the Tavern of Eternity

O merry hearts overcome
by music and pleasure,
ask wine from the player.
Surrender to the sound of the ney.

O you lucky, uplifted ones,
ride upon the horse of joy.
Sacrifice sorrow's steed
at the feet of good cheer.

O sober ones,
drink this wine from the jar of Union,
then destroy the mind
that always looks so far ahead of itself.

Spring has come.
There are hundreds of colors
in the rose garden and the meadow.
Forget those dark, cold winter months.

Open the ear of your soul.
Listen to the music
at the tavern of eternity.
Stop repeating the alphabet.

Fill your skull with that divine wine.
For God's sake,
roll up the covers of reason and the mind.

O lovers,
remove the garment of self-consciousness.
Annihilate yourself gazing
at the face of Immortal Beauty.

The Eggshell of the Body

If you want to feel rapture,
then give up thinking, and quit worrying.

You're like a bizarre bird in the shell of the
   body's egg.
You can't fly because you're inside the egg.

But when this egg is crushed,
you'll fly free and save your soul.

Open Your Door

If you could only open your door for a single
    moment,
you'd see everything and everyone
as a friend in your home.

At that moment, Jacob would see his son.
At that moment, the cupbearer of Union would
    serve you God's glorious wine.

That beauty would show his face and say,
"I am the one who sees you, who loves you.
Since you are open to my blessings,
you need no longer be afraid of anything."

No one there feels jealous of anyone else's
    attainments.
In the soul's garden, everyone is happy.

Heaven's Door

Your light is in my eye,
your beauty is in my heart.
God is my only sustenance.
Dear God, may my good fortune increase.

Forget about separation.
Respect and embrace each other.
Strive for Union.
Open the door of heaven.

Most people find hidden corners where they drink.
Not me. I drink openly, in front of everyone.

Reborn

"How come," Love said to me,
"You come around but don't stop by to see me?
I'm the one you want to see.

"I'm your house and your food.
I'm the one who caught your heart.
If you try to take your soul
away from me,
your soul becomes worthless.

"As long as you want only leaves,
you'll never know the fruits.
As long as you indulge yourself
with your own charms and graces,
you'll never know our charms and graces."

In every moment
you are reborn anew.
But the crowd of people doesn't know that.

Submerged in Absence

I have washed and cleaned the timber of being.
I have nothing more to do with this world.

My beloved keeps inviting me
to sit with him for a while.
I don't even pay attention to him,
So submerged am I in absence.

What can you say to one
who is not himself?
Crush my head a thousand times.
I couldn't care less.

Life Is Coming to the Rose Garden

O my soul,
warm spring breezes invite you
to the rose garden.

All the green leaves, the irises,
the tulips and hyacinths say,
"Whatever you sow,
that's what you'll harvest."

The roses have bloomed
to heal the pain of the thorns.
Water carries souls.
Life is coming back to the rose garden.

Leaves bring you news
of the fruits.
Don't scratch your head.
Come soon to the garden.

The Path in the Heart

The wonderful grape is the sultan of fruits
because its trunk is so lean.

During the winter of lust,
how long will the garden of our heart
stay imprisoned inside the fortress?

Look for the path in the heart,
O moonfaced soul.
What can you find in the earth
besides dust?

Get up. Wash your face.
But use the water
that makes the rose more beautiful.

The Rose's Plea

Rose sapling said to sweet basil,
"Put everything you have on our road."

"We are the prey for your traps,"
nightingale said to rose garden.

The rose turned to God's mercy and begged,
"Don't make this cold winter
your commandment to us."

God answered,
"How do you get the juice
without crushing?

"Don't worry about cold winter.
Sorrow and regrets
watch success arrive at my door.

"Gratitude, praise, and abundance
come only after you cry and beg."

Why Are You So Reasonable?

You are our soul.
You have the face of an angel.
You have given up all thoughts.

The one who gets lost in thought
is looking for a cure for his illness,
but thoughts themselves are the cause of his illness.

Reflection causes confusion.
Don't be a man of thought.
Stay pure and clean.
Become a man of joy and ecstasy instead.

Reason is a monster on this road.
O my soul,
become crazy, and go insane.
Why are you so reasonable?

The silkworm has many thoughts
and wants to parade his knowledge.
He does so by creating a cocoon
and kills himself in his confused ideas.

Be careful. Don't talk too much.
Stay silent.
You are not alone,
even so, try to stay silent.

You Are in His Hand

If you have headaches and troubles,
fall in love.
You'll free yourself
of all your pain and suffering.

If he blows on the ney a little stronger,
the salve will be placed on your eye,
and you'll be able to see the beloved's face.

You have fallen into the beloved's arm.
You are in his hand.
He carries you.

Don't ever reflect on the end.
You'll just become confused and lose your mind.

Cries of Confirmation

Adam carried a leather pouch for you.
Eve acted as Eve because of you.
But Adam and Eve weren't really the ones doing
    these things.
The Creator was acting through them.

Four rivers of absence
are in your glass.
Their majesty doesn't come from
the five senses and the six directions.

Scatter all of your particles in a single moment
so that cries of confirmation
fill the sky.

Words of the Secrets

The world is visible,
but its essence is secret.
The essence is its message.
The world is in the words.

A word comes from the heart
and has hundreds of faces.
Each face has a thousand strings.
Sounds come from them like music from a harp.

No words remain on the tongue,
but the heart is still filled by words.
The world vanishes,
but God remains.

The words of the secrets
that were revealed are now gone,
but their meaning lives on
in the heart.

Hidden from the Eyes

Our heart is our water bag.
Our body is our leather bottle.
They are placed on the back
of the water carrier.

He filled our stomachs from the fountain of soul.
Still, "Come, O thirsty one," he says.

The water carrier can't be seen,
but the water bag is right here.
Even so, the water carrier
never leaves his bag.

I am hidden from the eyes,
but watch what I do.
The smell of aloe wood is proof
that it is burning.

You Snatched My Heart

If you put your foot down and resist a little,
you'll save your head
and your worldly riches.
But if you surrender to love and lose your turban,
sixty new ones will come to you.

This is the whole fortune.
This is the whole glory.
This is the pleasure.
This is the life.
There can be no trading, no gain
besides this love.

My heart suddenly took me
to that imperial tent.
I was caught there.
So was my heart,
in a different way.

I asked him:
"You snatched my heart.
So where did you hide it?"
He said, "I didn't take it. Other pickpockets did."

"I'm afraid," I said to him.
"I need to ask the heart,
so no doubt remains."

"Tell the truth, O soul,
are there others besides you
who steal the heart?"

"Yes," he answered.
"They want to create temporary beauties."

They decorate the world with those beauties,
if new love and new ways do not come.

Every beauty restlessly looks,
day and night, for
new admirers of her beauty,
wherever there is a moonfaced
musk-fragrant one
who keeps searching for a crying lover.

At this moment, I'm his drunk.
Another day, I'll tell you new secrets
about a different subject.

Enough. Don't beat this drum
Because there are twenty others
at this rose garden
besides you.

The Moon's Slave

I am the slave of the moon.
It's the only thing I'm interested in.
So don't talk to me about anything other than
the moon, the candle, the sweetness of sugar.

Don't ever speak the word "trouble" out loud.
Talk to me only of treasure.
If you don't understand what I'm getting at,
then please leave me alone.

Cut It Short

You are wrapped up in the self from head to tail.
What are you looking for in yourself?
You're like water in the jug, encased in earthenware.

Embark on the journey of love.
It takes you from yourself to Yourself.
And cut the story short, my friend.

Songs of Heresy

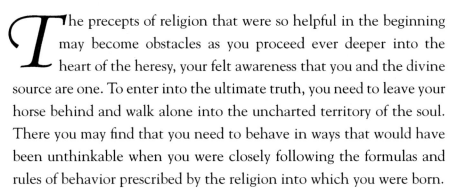

*T*he precepts of religion that were so helpful in the beginning may become obstacles as you proceed ever deeper into the heart of the heresy, your felt awareness that you and the divine source are one. To enter into the ultimate truth, you need to leave your horse behind and walk alone into the uncharted territory of the soul. There you may find that you need to behave in ways that would have been unthinkable when you were closely following the formulas and rules of behavior prescribed by the religion into which you were born.

The heretic loves God more than he or she loves religion. The heretic needs to be truer to his or her own visions and impulses than to those of the priests of the established religious order. How strange that your personal path to God often seems to be blocked or criticized by the priests of religion.

Do you dare break free of the confining rules? Do you dare to follow your own truth, even if it starts leading you astray from the path of your religion? What if this breaking free is the only way that you can really understand the truth of your religion? Can you follow the inner, heretical impulse even if it means risking your life to do so?

You Can't Get Away

You come and go,
look here and pass there.
You capture the hearts of beauties
and carry them away.

Don't try to run away, O heart.
You can't escape from him.

He doesn't open his door
until you become dust at his doorstep.
You can't pick up a rose
until the thorn has pricked you.

You can't get the ruby
if you don't dig in the mountain.
Unless you dive into the sea,
you can't find pearls or coral.

Your troubles will stay with you
until you become God's drunkard.
You can't capture Joseph of Canaan
unless you dress up like a wolf.

Too much comfort and good fortune
make the body soft and clumsy.

Without going through the troubles of religion,
you cannot reach the glory of faith.

Don't come confused to the Earth's bazaar,
and don't leave confused either.
In this business,
you can't get this
until you've given that.

What can I do?
Your face became the face of a beggar.
Nothing pleases you.
If you don't act like a heretic,
you can't reach the truth in Islam.

I Came Back to You

Come, O sweet-lipped beauty,
Drink this haram* wine
if you have the nerve.

If you have a heart like the sea,
pick up the wine that reveals
what being human is really about.

I came back to you
because I couldn't find the kind and decent things
I found in you anywhere else.

---

*Forbidden by religion.

Everyone Is Welcome to This School

Since the seminary of love
was endowed by eternity,
the difference between lover and Beloved
has become the most difficult subject.

There are other ways besides causality
and deductive reasoning to solve the problem.
But they're inaccessible to jurists, doctors,
and someone who fancies himself a cosmologist.

They all had strong opinions
and kept talking about their differences,
but it led only to a dead end.
Then, they turned toward the mosque,
but here everything became even more confused.

Thoughts are limited,
but the one who gathers them is endless.
Let what is limited disappear into the unlimited.

The fly of the soul has fallen into this buttermilk
    forever.
Muslim, Christian, Jew, and Zoroastrian:
All are welcome here.

You keep talking
but your words are like the fluttering wings of
   this fly.
Yet once the fly sinks to the bottom
its wings won't flutter anymore.

There is a better way for you to use your wings.
High above the dome of the sky
there is a new and invisible way for you to play.

A Stranger to Myself

Islam has come around so recently
yet Love has no beginning or end.
You can't call the unbeliever an infidel
if he's been the latest victim of Love.

O heart, listen to the song of the nightingale,
not the braying of the donkey.
O heart, go and loot the rose garden.
The thorns can't hurt you.

Enough. Stop beating the drum
and crafting words for others.
I've become a stranger to myself.
Please don't ask anything more of a stranger.

I Am the One!

My crazy heart is all tied up again,
but the real crazy is the one who has no idea
about the heart and has never felt its tugging.

I don't come from the earth or the sky,
nor from fire or water.
I became the One
whose name everybody takes an oath to.

I became Jesus to that moon.
I rose up and passed through the skies.
I am the drunk Moses.
God himself lives inside this patched cloak.

I'm crazy, insane, drunk out of my mind!
I don't listen to advice and deserve to be locked up.

I'm the tavern's rind. Why should I even be
    called a Sufi?
Who thinks a glass alone is enough?
Who can be happy with just one glass?

I've been falling up and down like a drunk,
rolling like a ball in the square.

I've been fully submerged and drawn into that sea.
Why should I just be a drop?
My heart and soul have come alive!
Why should I act as if I'm dead?

When Muhammad sees me drunk, my face pale,
he kisses my eyes, then I prostrate before him.

I am today's Muhammad, but not Muhammad of
    the past.
I am the phoenix of the time, not some small
    hungry bird.
I am the sultan of today, not yesterday's man.

Wake Up from Your Sleep

O people,
the books that kiraman katibin* wrote
fade away.
Wake up.
Go to work.
Start worshipping.

O God, correct us.
Have mercy on us.

He makes us smile after we've been crying.
Come, step forward through the curtain.
Wake up from your sleep.

---

*Angels who write about people's deeds, judging them as good or evil
(from the Koran 82-2).

He Is Beyond Praise

I haven't acquired my faith
in the power of the soul's beauty
through idle chatter.
I became his believer
only after I became my own infidel.

How long are you going to go on praising him?
He is beyond praise.
Enough. Be silent.
I go to my ecstasy.

Translator's Afterword

*S*ome of us are born restless, like misfits who are never satisfied by the offers of religion, science, and philosophy. Some of us don't want the comfort of conformity and tradition, so we accept the quest for truth as an individual journey that mirrors the process of our own death.

Self is the greatest enemy in this journey. Self is a hair in the eye, a thorn in the bottom of the soul's foot. Unless it is removed, none of us can see or walk. There won't be peace on earth until we all wage war against the self. When we become the martyr of our selves, then we conquer eternity.

Some of us believe creation has never taken place, that humanity is the child of perception, and the universe a hallucination. We are stuck in this world like a silkworm caged in its self-made cocoon. Seldom do we suspect that our limited perception put us in this predicament. Some of us believe there was no beginning, and that there is no end. If no one has ever been born, then no one ever dies.

Some of us also believe the answers to most of our questions (such as those about God, being, life, and death) are beyond our time- and space-bound perception. The great mystery is always in our realm. No one could franchise it, since the search for truth is the inborn nostalgia in all of us, at any time and at any place.

I am one of those restless misfits who became prey to Mevlana Jalaluddin Rumi, the man known to much of the world as Rumi, over 50 years ago. I found this world in 1928 and I have spent over thirty years translating into English all the volumes of the Turkish *Divan-i Kebir* prepared by Golpinarli, one of the most important Turkish scholars and admirers of Mevlana. Golpinarli's Turkish translation of the *Divan-i Kebir* is based on the 290-page divan, or anthology, handwritten by Hasan ibn Osman in 1368. This divan has 44,829 verses and 1,700 quatrains. It is registered under numbers 68 and 69 in the library of the Mevlana Museum in Konya, Turkey, and is located in a display case in the main hall of the museum.

I was fortunate to know Golpinarli before I left Turkey in 1956. Over the course of his life he authored more than a hundred books and translated all of Mevlana's works. Golpinarli passed away in 1982, having spent the last part of his life working at the Mevlana Museum. He was fluent in scholarly Arabic and Farsi and was familiar with the Mevlevi tradition through his family. He was familiar with all the divans and mesnevis (the other major literary work of Rumi) in the library of the museum. In fact, he prepared a descriptive catalog of all the manuscripts there. Golpinarli considered the divan he translated to be the most complete and reliable divan available. Although it is written in thirteenth-century Khorasani Farsi, the language spoken in Anatolia at the time, it also contains some Arabic, Turkish, and even Greek words and poems. Anyone who would like to try to read this original divan will appreciate the mixture.*

The Golpinarli divan has twenty-three volumes. I translated twenty-two of them, and these were published with the help and cooperation of the Turkish Ministry of Culture, to whom I am very grateful. I have now finished translating the remaining volume and approximately two hundred additional poems that don't belong to any standard volume. Reading these last poems of the divan is like walking through a minefield. One never knows which poem will blow the heart and mind. This kind of explosive experience is true for the divan as a whole, but even more so for these last poems, which show clearly how much at odds Mevlana was with the orthodox religious authority of his time.

How did Rumi get away with these words? His enormous popularity with the ordinary people, the maturity of the Seljuki palace, and the great confusion created by the invading Mongols in Anatolia may help explain some of that great mystery. The content of these poems, however, greatly complicated the job of getting them published eight hundred years later. Rumi does not reflect favorably in the eyes of present-day orthodox Islam, and the current Deputy Minister of Culture and Tourism in Turkey was not interested in copublishing the final volume of the divan.

Nevertheless, I thank him. Because of his reluctance, I was forced

---

*The Society for Understanding Mevlana (28 South Norfolk St., San Mateo, CA 94401) has a compact disc containing the microfilm of the original divan. The society is happy to send a copy of this divan to any Mevlana admirer or scholar. To purchase any of the initial twenty-two volumes of the *Divan-i Kebir*, visit www.sfumevlana.org.

to find cooperation elsewhere. I found it in my publisher, Inner Traditions, who helped bring this book into existence, and it is with them that I celebrate the completion of my goal. The poems appearing in this book are among my favorites from the last volume of the *Divan-i-Kebir*. My dear friend Will Johnson also helped me with the translations, and I'm grateful for the wonderful job he has done. Rumi's divine wine tastes better when it comes from Will's glass. I would also like to express my gratitude to Vicky Gersh for her generous help in preparing the original text.

Mevlana is like an immense ocean. There is something here for everyone, and his relevance to our time is greater now than ever. "Every prophet was praised by people of the same religion. Every master was loved by his disciples. But Mevlana is loved and respected by all nations and religions," said Ahmeddin Kayser, a high-ranking Seljuki government officer who died in 1284. This was Mevlana's miracle in the thirteenth century, and it still holds true in the twenty-first. But the importance of Mevlana goes far beyond religion and nationalism. His message is simple and clear to those who listen: "Come to me," he says. "I'll save you from yourself."

NEVIT O. ERGIN, M.D.
SAN MATEO, CALIFORNIA
JULY 2005